THANKS

your personal journal
of praise & promise

HARRIET BACSO

TreeTop Books
Nampa, Idaho

Scripture taken from the Holy Bible, New International Version. Copyright © 1973, 1978, 1984, International Bible Society. Used by permission of Zondervan Bible Publishers.

The extract credited to A. W. Tozer is from The Root of the Righteous, copyright © 1955, 1986. Used by permission of Christian Publications.

The extracts credited to Melody Beattie are from The Language of Letting Go, copyright © 1990. Used by permission of Hazelden Foundation.

The extract credited to Brother Lawrence and Frank Laubach is from Practicing His Presence, copyright © 1973. Used by permission of The Seed Sowers, Beaumont, TX.

Cover and interior design: Linda Criswell
Cover photo: Stan Sinclair

THANKS

TreeTop Books
PO Box 486
Nampa ID 83653-0486

ATTENTION SCHOOLS AND OTHER ORGANIZATIONS: This book is available at quantity discounts when purchased in bulk for fund raising or multiple gift giving.

ISBN: 0-9649008-0-7
Library of Congress Catalog Card Number: 95-61812
Printed in the United States of America
First printing: 1996

DEDICATION

to my three sons
Tim, JoeB, and Ken

and to my sweet friends
along the way

and to our God
Whom I simply thank

PREFACE

"I can't think of even ten things for which to be thankful," a close friend confided as we spoke in her comfortable home overlooking the mountains and vineyards of Napa Valley in California. Grey, bleak thoughts from personal circumstances distorted her view of God and erased the happiness in her life.

Upon returning to Idaho, my first inclination was to rush to the book store to look for additional help. Surely there must be a book that I could send her, something to help her focus on the joys in life. A secular book listing things to be happy about, some of them frivolous, sat on the shelves. But don't we as Christians have so much more for which to be grateful? That book didn't even mention the extravagant spiritual blessings of God. I'll make my own list, I concluded.

I read the entire Bible again, collecting my favorite happiness texts. For four years I've added to my list to total 7,000 things, and 700 Bible verses. This book, almost 3,000 things with about 300 Bible verses and 63 original poetic epigrams, is a condensation of that list.

Learning to give thanks more and more is delightful. I've found that the more I cherish the attitude of thankfulness, the higher my spirit soars. Depression lifts. Subtle joy replaces restlessness.

How about you? Do you find yourself in any one of the categories below? If you do, then this book is for you.

- grief recovery

- those who want an uplifting, encouraging book to give as gifts to others

- 12-step group members

- men and women who want to focus more on the positive effects of praise and thanksgiving in their prayers

- women's ministries

- anyone who wants to use thanks as a tool for emotional and spiritual progress

- those who simply want to fly high on gratitude

My prayer is that I'll meet each one of you in heaven where we'll thank Him forever and ever together. Always.   I'll see you there!

Quotes on Thanks from <u>The Language of Letting Go</u>
by Melody Beattie

"If we become stuck, miserable, feeling trapped and hopeless,
try gratitude . . .
If we have tried unsuccessfully to alter our present circumstances,
and have begun to feel like we're beating our head against a brick
wall, try gratitude . . .
If we feel like all is dark and the night will never end,
try gratitude . . .
If we feel scared and uncertain, try gratitude . . .
If we've tried everything else and nothing seems to work, try
gratitude . . .
If we've been fighting something, try gratitude . . .
When all else fails, go back to the basics. Gratitude . . ."

pp. 337, 338

"Gratitude turns negative energy into positive energy.
There is no situation or circumstance so small or large
that it is not susceptible to gratitude's power.
We can start with who we are and what we have today,
apply gratitude,
then let it work its magic.
Say thank you, until you mean it.
If you say it long enough, you will believe it."

p. 218

THANKS

Yes, we do live frenetic, busy lives. It seems as though there's never enough time, especially for ourselves and our own growth. It's easy, so easy, to cut ourselves short.

Let's try something different. Walk through the pages of this book with me. Discover the delights, pleasures, and happy results of simply giving thanks. Look at a few pages or only a few phrases -- it doesn't matter how long you read. Without structure or prescribed divisions in the book, whatever you read is right. Any length of time you spend is OK.

I've compiled a list of blessings for which I praise God. And I've sprinkled it with Bible texts from my personal studies. To give book universal appeal, I've overlooked potentially adverse topics such as holidays, spouses, children,

or many foods (I don't want to make you hungry for food as you read this --

just hungry for God).

So here's a "thank list" for you to amplify and personalize. Think about

each item. Highlight or underline your favorites. Ask yourself how this

might apply uniquely to you. Use the list as a springboard for personal prayer

and praise. Develop a passion for gratitude, fall in love with the attitude of

praise. Though the journal format invites you to write, it's OK just to

read . . . and think . . . and thank.

My hope is that you will interact with these things, that they will arouse

happy personal memories and thoughts, that you will make this your list, and

that you will revel in the fullness of joy found in praising and thanking God.

> "But as for me, I will always have hope;
> I will praise You more and more." Ps. 71:14

THANKS

God's gentleness
    "A bruised reed he will not break,
        and a smoldering wick he will not snuff out."
        Is. 42:3

12-step recovery programs

love
    "God is love." I John 4:16

the developing nations

being aware of God throughout the day
    "Fix your thoughts on Jesus." Heb. 3:1

happy times

    _____

    _____

    _____

God's invitation
    "Come and share your master's happiness!" Matt. 25:23

art museums

warm gloves on a frosty day

THANKS

a way out of deep depression
"Then they cried to the Lord in their trouble,
and he saved them from their distress.
He brought them out of darkness and the deepest gloom
and broke away their chains.
Let them give thanks to the Lord for his unfailing love
and his wonderful deeds for men."
Ps. 107:13-15

yellow forsythia saluting the arrival of spring

joy so deep it makes my heart hurt

that He teaches me
"I will instruct you and teach you in the way you should
go; I will counsel you and watch over you." Ps. 32:8

water faucets

drawing nearer to God

my joy in the Lord
"Rejoice in the Lord always.
I will say it again: Rejoice!"
Phil. 4:4

the equalizing laws of supply and demand

assistance

THANKS

expert advice
>"Plans fail for lack of counsel,
>>but with many advisers they succeed." Prov. 15:22

words warming my heart like sunshine

_____

_____

_____

autumn leaves crinkling beneath my feet

the moon rising over the city

a fair estimate

Christian radio stations and programs

wolf pups tussling playfully

the restorative qualities of happy dreams at night
>"At this I awoke and looked around.
>>My sleep had been pleasant to me." Jer. 31:26

dumping the clutter from my soul

a smoothly running engine

Thanks

supportive friends
>"I long to see you so that I may impart to you
>>some spiritual gift to make you strong." Rom. 1:11

avoiding disaster

the opening of a new store

building up endurance

changing leaves
>splashing my world
>>with dazzling hues and tones
>>>creating one last explosion of brilliance
>>>>before sleeping in brownness

each person making a contribution

a bouquet of flowers

bakeries

a vacation

that I can whistle in the dark
>"You are my hiding place;
>>you will protect me from trouble
>>>and surround me with songs of deliverance."
>Ps. 32:7

 HANKS

a winning smile

easy-to-follow instructions

hospitality
    "Do not forget to entertain strangers,
        for by so doing some people
            have entertained angels without knowing it."
          Heb. 13:2

old sadness banished

_____

_____

_____

wispy high cirrus clouds

the fever breaking

attending a religious conference or seminar

daylight

eating simply

bathroom fixtures

THANKS

salt
> "You are the salt of the earth." Matt. 5:13

the privilege of prayer

peppermint tea and honey

that God is my praise
> "He is your praise; he is your God,
> who performed for you those great
> and awesome wonders." Deut. 10:21

abstinence

the right equipment

electricity

a red amaryllis

fresh sheets on my bed

the splendor of God's creation

elegantly simple designs

the worldwide fellowship

making the best of crumby circumstances

THANKS

a sandy beach

the Sunday paper

memorizing Scripture while walking
        tucking God's Word in the channels of my mind
                detecting the patterns of His thoughts
                        contemplating the words and phrases
                                weaving them into the fabric of my life

continued growth

_____

_____

_____

clearance sales

wind freely blowing on the prairies

a free ticket

wild flowers in the woods

decisions based on the ultimate good rather than immediate want

browsing through unusual catalogs

THANKS

Jesus
        "For in Christ
                all the fullness of the Deity
                        lives in bodily form." Col. 2:9

the conversion of sunlight into electricity

reveling in His love
        "And I pray that you, being rooted and established
        in love, may have power . . . to grasp
                how wide
                      and long
                            and high
                                and deep
            is the love of Christ,
    and to know this love that surpasses knowledge --
        that you may be filled to the measure
                of all the fullness of God." Eph. 3:17-19

concern

outdoor trees aglow
        decorated with tiny white lights

a flock of Canadian geese
        winging their way northward
                behind a bold leader

editors

THANKS

high expectations

_____

_____

_____

emerald green

a flute's soulful lyrical sounds

home-care specialists

being better off than last year

sympathy
          "Carry each other's burdens."
                    Gal. 6:2

a special occasion

fair play

eye contact

coping with the stresses of contemporary life

buying bulk items

health
> "Dear friend, I pray that you may enjoy good health
> and that all may go well with you,
> even as your soul is getting along well."
> III John 2

that God is my security when tempted
> "The name of the Lord is a strong tower;
> the righteous run to it and are safe." Prov. 18:10

correcting my own mistakes

the rejuvenating experience of knowing Christ
> "Come to me, all you who are weary and burdened,
> and I will give your rest.
> Take my yoke upon you and learn from me,
> for I am gentle and humble in heart
> and you will find rest for your souls
> For my yoke is easy and my burden is light." Matt. 11:28-30

familiar melodies and words

_____

_____

_____

the dry cleaners

THANKS

blenders

living in harmony

a sense of purpose

taking off my stiff mask
        and revealing my real self

changing my mind

that the danger has passed

a sensitive conscience

crossing unnecessary items off the list

bold plans

_____

_____

_____

teachers of the Word
        "Those who are wise will instruct many." Dan. 11:33

warmth in winter

a short airport concourse

common sense

becoming uncomplicated outwardly
      so I can enjoy more peace within

the city outlined against the silvery edge of night

Bible concordances

asserting the truth

for God speaking eloquently through me
      "Do not worry beforehand about what to say.
            Just say whatever is given you at the time,
                for it is not you speaking,
                    but the Holy Spirit." Mark 13:11

daring to take a risk for a noble cause

protection
      "Spread your protection over them,
            that those who love your name may rejoice in you."
          Ps. 5:11

the common thread of faith in God linking the centuries

birds optimistically singing in the predawn grey

THANKS

God's personal gifts to me

_____

_____

_____

_____

_____

_____

THANKS

our daily food

summer

the conversion of a mean person into a compassionate one

books on tape

God's guidance
> "This is what the Lord says:
>> 'Stand at the crossroads and look;
>>> ask for the ancient paths,
>>>> ask where the good way is, and walk in it,
> and you will find rest for your souls.'" Jer. 6:16

other church denominations

cameras

making more space

fulfilling someone's quiet needs
> "A friend loves at all times." Prov. 17:17

a shortcut

warm tranquil August evenings

black elegant dinnerware

THANKS

carolers singing at my door or in the mall

reasons for joy
> "I delight greatly in the Lord;
>> my soul rejoices in my God.
>>> For he has clothed me with garments of salvation
>>>> and arrayed me in a robe of righteousness."
>>>> Is. 61:10

debriefing with someone who cares after a tough experience

the cooing of a dove

tearing down a wall between us
> "For he himself is our peace,
>> who has made the two one and has destroyed the barrier,
>>> the dividing wall of hostility." Eph. 2:14

our constitution guaranteeing us "the pursuit of happiness"

tiger swallowtail butterflies

capitalism

the breath of life

beeswax candles

coming out of an accident without a scratch

Thanks

the reciprocity of giving
"Cast your bread upon the waters,
for after many days you will find it again."
Eccl. 11:1

cheerful people

_____

_____

_____

our ethnic differences

thinking about the billions of galaxies in space

car pools

serenity

getting free of excesses
"Why spend money on what is not bread,
and your labor on what does not satisfy?
Listen, listen to me, and eat what is good,
and your soul will delight
in the richest of fare." Is. 55:2

delicate colors

THANKS

childlike spontaneous trust

that Jesus is always with me
      "And surely I am with you always,
            to the very end of the age." Matt. 28:20

celebrating a baptism

the Beatitudes (Matt. 5:3-12)

dense green grass

choosing to distract my mind from the temptation

the ability to think
      "'Come now, let us reason together,' says the Lord."
        Is. 1:18

a rare opportunity

_____

_____

_____

dependable transportation

Christian characteristics

 $\mathscr{T}$HANKS

congratulations

hugs from God
>"You hem me in -- behind and before;
>>you have laid your hand upon me.
>>>Such knowledge is too wonderful for me,
>>>>too lofty for me to attain." Ps. 139:5

determination

the realization that I want to appreciate life's common moments now
>"Show me, O Lord, my life's end and the number of my days;
>>let me know how fleeting is my life."
>>>Ps. 39:4

chubby rosy-faced cherubs

a falafel sandwich

heaven
>"I am going there to prepare a place for you . . .
>>I will come back and take you to be with me
>>>that you also may be where I am." John 14:2,3

celebrating a birthday

a quick refreshing 10-minute catnap

dimples

Thanks

the visibility through cellophane wrapping

gaiety
　　　"You have filled my heart with greater joy
　　　　　than when their grain and new wine abound."
　　　　　　　Ps. 4:7

brightly colored socks

facing the truth about a situation
　　　"Then you will know the truth,
　　　　　and the truth will set you free." John 8:32

sparkling bathrooms

firsthand information

the protection of angels
　　　"'Don't be afraid,' the prophet answered.
　　　　　'Those who are with us are more than
　　　　　　　those who are with them.'" II Kings 6:16

changing a strained relationship into a warm joyous one

breaking free

the tropical rain forest

clear decisive evidence

Thanks

Prayers answered

_____

_____

_____

_____

_____

_____

_____

that Jesus thinks we're worth it all
"After the suffering of his soul,
he will see the light (of life) and be satisfied."
Is. 53:11

childhood friends

_____

_____

_____

fixing my eyes on Jesus

the refreshing effect of God's word on my life
"Let my teaching fall like rain
and my words descend like dew,
like showers on new grass,
like abundant rain on tender plants." Deut. 32:2

Christ controlling each facet of my life

delivery from personal pain

reciprocal love
"May the Lord make your love increase and overflow
for each other and for everyone else,
just as ours does for you." I Thes. 3:12

flights that arrive on time

a time when I checked just to be sure

balance in caring for myself and caring for others

comfortable cotton clothes

dependable day care

being open and honest
  "You know we never used flattery,
    nor did we put on a mask to cover up greed--
     God is our witness." I Thes. 2:5

Christian education

the privilege of asking
  "Ask and it will be given to you;
    seek and you will find;
     knock and the door will be opened to you."
    Matt. 7:7

changing an upsetting circumstance with a smile

flushing toilets

committing my life to Christ

detecting the flaw beforehand

THANKS

eyes
      "The eye is the lamp of the body.
          If your eyes are good,
               your whole body will be full of light." Matt. 6:22

church bells ringing

benevolence
      "Do everything in love." I Cor. 16:14

clarifying a misunderstanding

the triumphant haunting yowls of coyotes at night

giving away my extra things around the house

humility
      "The fear of the Lord teaches a man wisdom,
          and humility comes before honor." Prov. 15:33

Christ in me

keeping it simple

a positive attitude

complementary colors

bright ideas

that it's OK if some don't like me
    "If people do not welcome you,
        shake the dust off your feet
           when you leave their town." Luke 9:5

a peaceful night

the freedom to express my honest feelings

celebrations

_____

_____

_____

glowing autumn trees

discount stores

experienced workers

that this earth is not my permanent home
    "But our citizenship is in heaven.
        And we eagerly await a Savior from there,
           the Lord Jesus Christ." Phil. 3:20

conquering those fears

THANKS

bargains

the tenderness of a mother mule deer with her spotted fawn

clasping hands cordially

diving right into that enormous task

clinics to help

beach umbrellas

doing it on the spur of the moment

the Orion Nebula --
      a brilliantly colorful place in the sky
           with a vast curved tunnel illuminated by light
                where new stars and suns are continuously created

ample room for stuff

a songbird's trill

cleaning even one closet or drawer

growing more and more sensitive
      to the guidance of the Holy Spirit

making a will even for my modest estate

comfortable daily routines

_____

_____

_____

beautiful watercolor paintings

the sounds of the forest

an anonymous gift or surprise

getting rid of the burden and heavy baggage of sin
 "Let us throw off everything that hinders
  and the sin that so easily entangles,
   and let us run with perseverance
    the race marked out for us." Heb. 12:1

completing a project on time

a fresh breeze

burled wood

dressing up

photographs

THANKS

angels' missions
>"While I was still in prayer, Gabriel . . .
>came to me in swift flight . . .
>He instructed me and said to me,
>'Daniel, I have now come to give you
>insight and understanding.'"
>Dan. 9:21,22

contagious optimism

persistence
>"We have come to share in Christ
>if we hold firmly till the end
>the confidence we had at first." Heb. 3:14

an even temperament

the showy colorful flowers of cactus in bloom

a smooth flow of traffic

an honest relationship free from deception

consecrating my life to Christ

that God is my delight
>"God, my joy and my delight." Ps. 43:4

medical science

letting my life shine
        "His face was radiant
                because he had spoken with the Lord." Ex. 34:29

making the right choice

_____

_____

_____

a friendly church

liberality
        "But just as you excel in everything . . .
                see that you also excel in this grace of giving."
                II Cor. 8:7

networking with the right people

a good character
        "Wisdom is proved right by her actions." Matt. 11:19

combs and brushes

an up-close view

dignity

THANKS

feeling at ease with God
 "We know that we belong to the truth . . .
  we set our hearts at rest in his presence." I John 3:19

continuing my education

a hot and cold shower

buying groceries

mixed emotions
 "So the women hurried away from the tomb,
  afraid yet filled with joy." Matt. 28:8

the orderly harmonious cosmos

another hug

memories that bring a smile

_____

_____

_____

cooperation

a little extra to fall back on

# THANKS

more happy mornings

diminishing the risk

complying with the guidelines

an understanding look

Calvary
> "But he was pierced for our transgressions,
>   he was crushed for our iniquities;
> the punishment that brought us peace was upon him,
>   and by his wounds we are healed." Is. 53:5

being set free

words of kindness

a reasonable cost of living

fidelity

candid and straightforward words
> "The pleasantness of one's friend
>   springs from his earnest counsel." Prov. 27:9

Mother Teresa and others like her

easy access

THANKS

joy in His presence
> "You will fill me with joy in your presence,
> with eternal pleasures at your right hand."
> Ps. 16:11

music

_____

_____

_____

finding a way

my adaptability

corroborating the truth by evidence

fellowship
> "They . . . ate together with glad and sincere hearts,
> praising God and enjoying the favor of all the people."
> Acts 2:46

energizing ideas

ladybugs

the right to determine my own future to a large extent

Thanks

my favorite food

countless opportunities to do good deeds for others

the words "it was benign"

a fresh spring day

the splendor of embossed book covers

crying a little

high mesas and deep canyons

seven

the surging, crashing, roaring ocean waves

my material blessings

_____

_____

_____

credit cards used carefully

the treelined oval on campus

 Thanks

hanging on
  "Love the LORD your God,
    listen to his voice,
      and hold fast to him.
  For the LORD is your life." Deut. 30:20

a cup of cool water

leaving old ways
  "One thing I do: Forgetting what is behind
    and straining toward what is ahead,
  I press on toward the goal to win the prize
    for which God has called me heavenward
      in Christ Jesus." Phil. 3:13,14

courtesy

my own desk

fields of grain as far as the eye can see

thank-you cards

clothes that fit

generosity
  "A poor widow put in two very small copper coins.
   '. . . this poor widow has put in more
    than all the others.'" Luke 21:2,3

hungering for a closer relationship with God
  "O God, you are my God,
    earnestly I seek you;
      my soul thirst for you,
        my body longs for you,
  in a dry and weary land where there is no water." Ps. 63:1

curing that illness through natural methods

that day follows night

ability to appraise a precarious situation with calmness

colorful bed linen

that it'll be OK
  "All things God works for the good of those who love him,
    who have been called according to his purpose."
    Rom. 8:28

needed advice

_____

_____

_____

a moment of sheer beauty

THANKS

more and more love
> "And this is my prayer:
>> that your love may abound more and more
>>> in knowledge and depth of insight." Phil. 1:9

that it didn't take much coaxing

childlike faith

gothic cathedrals with tall spires and pointed arches

letting others comfort me

forever

emotional recovery

my thoughts

a mug of steaming cocoa

the determination to do God's will no matter what
> "I will go to the king,
>> even though it is against the law.
>>> And if I perish, I perish." Esther 4:16

a reason to visit

that my destiny is in God's hands

less stress

"Do not be anxious about anything,
but in everything, by prayer and petition,
with thanksgiving, present your requests to God."
Phil. 4:6

chaste and modest conduct

glinting waves on a lake

a cushioned chair

singing songs aloud when I'm home alone

that a formidable problem is solved with God's help

_____

_____

_____

being complete in Jesus

the ability of the human body to repair injury

checking out books from the library

exploring country roads on a bicycle

a decade of relative prosperity

charity
>   "For where you treasure is,
>   there your heart will be also."
>   Luke 12:34

exponential growth

plain ordinary moments

the beauty of simplicity

dividing the work equally

help in prayer
>   "The Spirit helps us in our weakness.
>   We do not know what we ought to pray for,
>   but the Spirit himself intercedes for us
>   with groans that words cannot express."
>   Rom. 8:26

covering all the bases

dropping off to sleep quickly

each snowflake's intricate design

crepe paper in dazzling colors

that recovery follows grief

being safe inside my home
        as sheets of rain slice the darkness
            as thunder roars and trembles
                as lightning flashes threateningly

doing what I've always wanted to do

_____

_____

_____

each day of the week

a drive in the country

facing the future with confidence

that I am special
        "But you are a chosen people, a royal priesthood, a holy
            nation, a people belonging to God, that you may declare
              the praises of him." I Pet. 2:9

fastening my hope on Christ

ears

THANKS

keeping on
> "Perseverance must finish its work." James 1:4

curiosity

dancing spontaneously for joy

geese honking as they fly south on a grey autumn day

exchanging bondage for freedom of soul

a gift-basket of citrus fruits

safety
> "He will cover you with his feathers,
>   and under his wings you will find refuge."
>   Ps. 91:4

dewdrops

color photography

daubing a bit of matching paint on my car's small scratch

exhilarating people

faith in tomorrow

elasticity

Thanks

Thoughts about seasons

_____

_____

_____

_____

_____

_____

_____

Thanks

a happy ending

canary yellow

blood banks

days between seasons when it's neither hot nor cold

God's leading
> "In his heart a man plans his course,
> but the Lord determines his steps." Prov. 16:9

deciding to live my life in His service wherever I am

finding the real cause of a problem

_____

_____

_____

eliminating possible complications

pink satin ribbon

a little more courage

contact lenses

book sales at the airport

getting through the grief process
　　　"Blessed are those who mourn,
　　　　　　for they will be comforted." Matt. 5:4

deep purple

an intimate awareness of God
　　　here with me
　　　　　　throughout the day

emotional healing

bouncing back to health after an illness

a pat on the back

kindness
　　　"Do to others what you would have them do to you."
　　　　　Matt. 7:12

declaring my real feelings

exploring small boutiques

fluffy yellow chicks cheeping

lustrous washable silk

THANKS

delegating part of the responsibilities to others

fountains spraying and playing

a beautiful day

endurance

dressing down

bravery

energetic devotion to God

crackling campfires

eloquent words
> "For I will give you words and wisdom
> that none of your adversaries
> will be able to resist or contradict."
> Luke 21:15

making a difference

brilliant composers and musicians

a beautifully composed photo

drive-ins

THANKS

the breathtaking intimacy in knowing God

perfume
> "Perfume and incense bring joy to the heart."
> Prov. 27:9

eternal truths

_____

_____

_____

marching to a different drummer if I choose

each culture

a direct route

curious playful kittens

everyone carrying his/her share of the load

meeting a friend in a shopping mall

fitting in/standing out

daydreaming a little

46

Thanks

the only true Source of peace
"My soul finds rest in God alone;
my salvation comes from him."
Ps. 62:1

money-saving offers

exercising in the open air

flexible schedules

tears of joy

calculators '

promises
"And about the matter you and I discussed --
remember, the Lord is witness
between you and me forever." I Sam. 20:23

a better understanding

florists

applesauce on toast or pancakes

shiny yellow buttercups blooming in an open meadow

mutual respect

chastity/purity
> "Do not arouse or awaken love
> until it so desires." Song 2:7

books

_____

_____

_____

my Counselor
> "He will give you another Counselor to be with you
> forever. " John 14:16

flying high

cows moving closer to the fence to watch me as I walk by

arriving ahead of time

everyday life

compatible people

oranges

a fair game

 *Thanks*

morning devotions
    "Very early in the morning,
        while it was still dark,
            Jesus got up,
                left the house
    and went off to a solitary place,
        where he prayed." Mark 1:35

for Jesus by my side

artful buffet salads

establishing a new good habit

_____

_____

_____

sweet deep sleep

my body's conversion of food into energy

covering the tomato plants just one more time before frost

automatic door openers in stores

bold intense designs

filling my thoughts with good things

learning to see God
        in everybody and everything
          all around me

that God is easily approachable

avoiding a crash

finding an old diary

God's healing love

my craving for God
        "How lovely is your dwelling place, O Lord Almighty!
         My soul yearns, even faints,
            for the courts of the Lord;
         my heart and my flesh cry out
            for the living God." Ps. 84:1,2

Christian TV programs

a silky mist rising from
      a lake
          a field
              or a valley

breaking isolation

THANKS

going to lunch with a friend

balloon bouquets

finishing my calisthenics for the day

cotton puffs of cirrocumulus clouds dotting the sky

bright happy Chinese lanterns

intercessory prayer --
       entering with God into His experience
            of love and concern for others

that I can give to worthy charities

my most valued possession

_____

_____

_____

good daily decisions

bean burritos
       smothered with hot salsa
            lettuce, onions and tomatoes

the gift of Jesus
> "Thanks be to God for his indescribable gift!"
> II Cor. 9:15

fitting all the pieces together

the joy in bringing someone to Christ

my desire to make God look good
> "Then the nations will know that I am the Lord . . .
> when I show myself holy through you before their eyes."
> Ezek. 36:23

phoning a friend

braces

flexible people

cafeterias

intelligence
> "'Call to me and I will answer you and tell you
> great and unsearchable things
> you do not know.'" Jer. 33:3

placing my confidence in God

a demonstration on how to use a new product

THANKS

the ocean
> "The sea is his, for he made it."
> Ps. 95:5

calla lilies

feeling refreshed as I awaken

happy memories

_____

_____

_____

the miracle of mornings

plump orange persimmons ripening on my kitchen counter

my wonderful Higher Power

eliminating the extra duties
　　and unnecessary details
　　　　that press on my mind
　　　　　　so I can make more time
　　　　　　　　for Him

fortifying my life with memory texts

colors everywhere
> from the dazzling fish of the sea's coral reefs
> > to the sweeping display of a sunset;
> from the microscopic components of life
> > to the planets billions of light years away;
> color pervades every detail of creation
> > as an extraordinary gift of ecstasy from God!

no-iron clothes

former doubts being swept away

letting go of a damaging relationship

contented cows grazing in a lush pasture

my pillow

light lyrical soothing music

prompt refunds

eyeglasses

freedom of speech

the intricate chemical complexities within even one cell

doing it the right way

THANKS

fresh cut Shasta daisies

my desire to serve
> "Then I heard the voice of the Lord saying,
> 'Whom shall I send? And who will go for us?'
> And I said, 'Here am I. Send me!'"
> Is. 6:8

sharing an intimate anxiety with God

_____

_____

_____

public education for all

that God is always available

clusters of blue Colorado columbine in mountain meadows

the instinctive maps within migrating birds

friendly cashiers

listening with my heart

putting my best foot forward

knowing that I'm in God's loving embrace
    "As the mountains surround Jerusalem,
        so the Lord surrounds his people
           both now and forevermore." Ps. 125:2

going somewhere new

finding it easy

cordiality

my familiarity with the Bible

good character traits

_____

_____

_____

the vast expanse of the universe

lovely gift-wrapping paper

an active living faith
    "Faith by itself,
        if it is not accompanied by action,
          is dead." James 2:17

Thanks

corresponding with life-long friends

overcoming anxiety

gentle words

_____

_____

_____

happiness at work
"Whatever you do, work at it with all your heart,
as working for the Lord, not for men,
since you know that you will receive
an inheritance from the Lord as a reward.
It is the Lord Christ you are serving."
Col. 3:23,24

clues to the solution of a nasty problem

flying a kite

cleanliness
"Let us purify ourselves
from everything that contaminates body and spirit,
perfecting holiness out of reverence for God.
II Cor. 7:1

pausing to listen to sounds of nature

colored glass

people concerned enough to do something

flowers in window boxes

education
> "Let the wise listen and add to their learning,
>   and let the discerning get guidance-- . . .
> The fear [love] of the Lord
>   is the beginning of knowledge." Prov. 1:5,7

glorious sunshine

a meaningful excerpt from my favorite book

_____

_____

_____

getting involved in helping others

personality tests

focusing on thankfulness

THANKS

Relationships to pray for

_____

_____

_____

_____

_____

_____

_____

God's power and love flowing through me
"'Whoever believes in me . . .
streams of living water will flow from with him.'"
John 7:38

clear directions

growth

keeping informed of current events

inspiring words
"And let us consider how we may spur one another on
toward love and good deeds." Heb. 10:24

gift certificates

a new stirring within myself for more closeness with God

comfort in the silent presence of another

dedication

perfection
"'My grace is sufficient for you,
for my power is made perfect in weakness.'"
II Cor. 12:9

keeping the lines of communication open

coming to a stop in the nick of time

the faintly colored corona around the moon on a hazy night

gentle and kind words
       "A word aptly spoken
            is like apples of gold in settings of silver."
               Prov. 25:11

knowing I can always count on my friend

for God filling this moment

off-white

practical information

laundry detergents

my early Christian experience
       "Remember those earlier days
           after you had received the light,
               when you stood your ground." Heb. 10:32

God's all-embracing love

open spaces

competitive prices

pressing onward

learning a new song

case dismissed because the opposition didn't show

fixing it

basking in the sunlight of His love all day
"Satisfy us in the morning with your unfailing love,
that we may sing for joy and be glad all our days."
Ps. 90:14

the delicate beauty of transparent dragonfly wings

good financial advice

_____

_____

_____

a pocket edition of the Bible

my favorite shirt

letter openers

the ministry of music
  "Speak to one another with
    psalms,
      hymns
        and spiritual songs.
  Sing and make music in your heart to the Lord,
    always giving thanks to God the Father for everything,
      in the name of our Lord Jesus Christ."
        Eph. 5: 19,20

God's nearness

putting a bandage on a blister

silvery shafts of moonlight penetrating the darkness of my room

gentle thoughts

flickering candlelight

positive feedback

an attitude of gratitude

church fellowship
  "But I am like an olive tree
    flourishing in the house of God . . .
  I will praise you in the presence of your saints."
    Ps. 52:8,9

quiet times

paying attention to my own needs

my personal growth

cash discounts

brilliantly-hued tropical fish

reading a favorite book again

the life-giving words of the Bible
        "He said to them, 'Take to heart all the words
            I have solemnly declared to you . . .
                    They are not just idle words for you --
                        they are your life." Deut. 32:46,47

greeting cards

God's companionship

my wealth, great or small

ready-made bows

happy songs
        "Sing the glory of his name;
            make his praise glorious!" Ps. 66:2

THANKS

listening to the rain

faithfulness

expressing thanks

_____

_____

_____

nature's winsome creatures

recognizing an inaudible cry for help

for God filling the void in my heart

birds greeting the sunrise with notes of ecstasy

following in His footsteps

extra encouragement

new behavior

my brain -- my miraculous computer system center

letting it wait until tomorrow/doing it now

close spiritual bonding with one another and God
>	"Two are better than one . . .
>	If one falls down, his friend can help him up . . .
>	Though one may be overpowered, two can defend themselves.
>	A cord of three strands is not quickly broken."
>	Eccl. 4:9,10,12

for God speaking in quietness

exuberance

my Help
>	"I can do everything through him who gives me strength."
>	Phil. 4:13

remembering to take the camera

the conversion of desert into fertile land through irrigation

fundamental strong religious beliefs

God's love in every ordinary moment

liking who I am

reverent silence

gold

THANKS

bean bag games

the wondrous healing abilities of the human body

my most comfortable shoes

looking at the overall picture

feeding ducks in the park

God's personal attention to me
       "You are precious and honored in my sight,
            and . . . I love you." Is. 43:4

thinking about the sacrifice of Jesus on the cross for me

all fifty states

lower fees

bales of hay in a field

the aroma of fresh bread in the oven

all the facts

rich texture

mail forwarding

Thanks

gentle chords of music

baptism

> "And now what are you waiting for?
>   Get up, be baptized
>   and wash your sins away, calling on his name."
>   Acts 22:16

feeling comfortable enough to cry with a friend

running on the beach

sampling cologne in a store

meeting a challenge

reading a poem

monarch butterflies

quiet truths cherished deep within my heart

_____

_____

_____

getting into the auditorium in spite of the crowds

my invitation to the heavenly banquet
       "Blessed are those who are invited
              to the wedding supper of the Lamb!" Rev. 19:9

happy laughing music

communicating easily

a heart full of love

light fleecy snow

getting through a painful passage

clearing away the junk in my life
       that blocks my view of God

seedless grapes

aromatic clusters of lily of the valley

handling problems well

realistic replicas

God's plans for me
       "'For I know the plans I have for you,' declares the Lord,
         'plans to prosper you and not to harm you,
            plans to give you hope and a future.'" Jer. 29:11

lingering later into the evening

that God admires me
        "Wait till the Lord comes . . .
             At that time each will receive
                 his praise from God." I Cor. 4:5

hot water upon demand in my home

the change in the weather

recognizing and keeping a confidence

peaceful sleep
        "I will lie down and sleep in peace,
            for you alone, O Lord, make me dwell in safety."
           Ps. 4:8

music that coaxes my cares away

getting to know a casual acquaintance better

the complicated chemical reactions in our world

listening to the silence

breaking off an unhealthy relationship

ice cream cones

scenes of my childhood

_____

_____

_____

regular rhythms of rest and exercise

the joy of salvation
          "He was filled with joy
                    because he had come to believe in God." Acts 16:34

January -- when the new year pulsates with promise

love and laughter saving the day

an iridescent rainbow trout gliding through clear water

interior decorators

catching up my correspondence

replacing falsehood with truth

my best friend

bronze statues

Thanks

juice in individual disposable cartons

rhythms of life on a city street

plans moving along like clockwork

caffeine-free soft drinks

my enthusiasm for life

inner healing
> "When we were overwhelmed by sins,
> you forgave our transgressions." Ps. 65:3

exploring antique stores

thirsty paper towels

expressions of caring

the barren stark beauty of the badlands

doing something special for myself

_____

_____

_____

orchards dotting the landscape

doing my best
      "Let your light shine before men,
            that they may see your good deeds
                 and praise your Father in heaven." Matt. 5:16

rich wood grains

feeling fine

competition in the marketplace

people of every description

allowing God's love to grow in me
      "There is no fear in love.
            But perfect love drives out fear ."
          I John 4:18

the wind softly humming through a pine forest

calling it a day

a friendly disposition

running to God in my disappointments

being enveloped in God's love

knowing God
    "Now this is eternal life: that they may know you,
        the only true God,
           and Jesus Christ,
              whom you have sent." John 17:3

condensed books

getting better, not worse, with age

satisfying experiences

cobalt blue

an abundant crop from the vegetable garden

ethnic foods

_____

_____

_____

school buses

colored sheets of paper

exceeding even my own expectations

THANKS

insight-filled meditations

the barely-risen sun sleeping for a moment on the horizon

easy terms

a safe trip

self-assurance

food stores that are open around the clock

insight
> "If any of you lacks wisdom, he should ask God,
> who gives generously to all without finding fault,
> and it will be given to him." James 1:5

a moist orange slice

newly forged bonds of friendship

peace of mind
> "You will keep in perfect peace
> him whose mind is steadfast,
> because he trusts in you." Is. 26:3

my home

cheerfulness

THANKS

an eloquent speech

exoneration

God
> "Before me no god was formed,
> nor will there be one after me.
> I, even I, am the Lord,
> and apart from me there is no savior.
> Yes, and from ancient days I am he."
> Is. 43:10,11,13

eliminating discrimination

not allowing a busy schedule to crowd out my time with God

immersing myself in a good cause

a fresh fruit dessert

all my tomorrows

decreasing the chances of failure

refreshing thoughts

emerging from trouble unharmed

almonds

Thanks

the interactive Trinity
 "At that time Jesus,
  full of joy through the Holy Spirit, said,
   'I praise you, Father, Lord of heaven and earth.'"
    Luke 10:21

a white waterfall cascading over a cliff

interviews with deeply spiritual people

the words "no artificial flavors"

endless heavenly ecstasy

facing the future with new confidence

ambition

wholesome recreation

_____

_____

_____

engrossing prayer

a decent wage

expecting the best in others

peace with God
      "Since we have been justified through faith,
            we have peace with God through our Lord Jesus Christ."
                  Romans 5:1

keeping a diary or personal journal

an agreeable settlement of a dispute

my flexible fingers

expertise

enlarging the scope of my understanding

a fresh start every morning
      "His compassions never fail.
            They are new every morning."
                  Lam. 3:22,23

our high calling to represent Christ to others

slipping away for some quiet time

fine workmanship

common ground

Christians
   "Go! This man is my chosen instrument
      to carry my name." Acts 9:15

exposing a false rumor

the back roads

overnight delivery

a little luxury

my feet

small daily miracles

_____

_____

_____

cloudy days

a dependable car

five senses

two friends

THANKS

the principle that by beholding we become changed

keeping costs down

snugly cotton flannel sheets

preserving my selfhood

unconditional love

that God's love moved Him to be one of us
  "The Word became flesh and made his dwelling among us.
    We have seen his glory, the glory of the One and Only,
      who came from the Father, full of grace and truth."
      John 1:14

economizing effectively

the privilege of tenderly caring for someone who's dying

keeping secrets

soft mauves and purples

public broadcasting stations

a clothes dryer

extending the deadline

THANKS

a Christlike character
"Clothe yourselves with the Lord Jesus Christ."
Rom. 13:14

the release of forgiveness

Kleenex

fragrant purple lilac blossoms

solving a complicated problem

pushing back the boundaries of my world

uplifting entertainment

energy efficient homes

simply saying thanks

_____

_____

_____

the songs of birds

laughing at myself

checking accounts

quiet miracles

a good reputation
"A good name is more desirable than great riches;
to be esteemed is better than silver or gold."
Prov. 22:1

visual rhythm

the sudden collapse of communism in USSR and Eastern Bloc nations

spring

re-creation in our hearts

walking with God in success and happy times

the systematic cycles of life

learning something new

that He nourishes the real needs of my soul
"I am the living bread that came down from heaven.
If anyone eats of this bread,
he will live forever." John 6:51

starting the day with a smile

Thanks

reading the Bible in the course of a year

empathy
       "'Lord, . . . if you had been here,
             my brother would not have died.'
      When Jesus saw her weeping . . .
           he was deeply moved in spirit and troubled . . .
               Jesus wept." John 11:21,33-35

helpful brochures and pamphlets

a unique original work of art

reflections in still water

cat's-eye marbles

the amazingly tiny hummingbird hovering above a flower

strength for each day

high intensity electric colors

inner calm
      "A heart at peace gives life to the body." Prov. 14:30

simple techniques

a shopping trip

studying other civilizations

red tulips stretching towards the warmth of the sun

honesty

the ability to decide

sunshine in the storm

a good credit rating

the hot air balloon fiesta in Albuquerque

remembering that special time

_____

_____

_____

a feeling of adventure

achieving beyond my usual

sleeping in

taking a chance

composing a poem

an etiquette book

experiencing feelings of wellness

Belgian waffles

a scampering squirrel

the influence of friends
      "He who walks with the wise grows wise." Prov. 13:20

connecting a face with a name

gifts
      "Every good and perfect gift is from above,
            coming down from the Father of the heavenly lights."
                  James 1:17

an extra treat

that I can pay my bills

each of my brain cells

chrysanthemums

a bluer-than-blue sky

consumer credit

the aeolian sound from an ocean shell

an open door

Easter lilies

a card of encouragement at just the right time

contemporary Christian music

an unexpected dividend or rebate

eating my corn on the cob raw for a nice change of taste

classical books

contributing my point of view

brightly-colored sailboats

another chance

a pleasure I savor again and again

certificates of deposit

bird feeders

odds and ends

_____

_____

_____

antibiotics

elation

the incredible complexity of the human body
"I praise you because I am fearfully and wonderfully made;
your works are wonderful, I know that full well."
Ps. 139:14

black

copyrights

antique furniture

recharging my spiritual energy

impartiality
"He causes his sun to rise on the evil and the good,
and sends rain on the righteous and unrighteous."
Matt. 5:45

Thanks

a museum of natural history

more fun for less money

extroverts/introverts

graciousness

the harmonious laws of God
pulsating through the universe

clear corneas in my eyes

parting company with those that would drag me down

flextime in the workplace

that God sought me to be one of His own
"I will show my love
to the one I called 'Not my loved one.'
I will say to those called 'Not my people,'
'You are my people';
And they will say,
'You are my God.'"
Hosea 2:23

factual information

green, yellow and red bell peppers

Thanks

high standards

colorful charts and graphs

Handel's <u>Messiah</u>

remembering a special smile

a robin darting in and out of a tree as she builds her nest

food enough in the kitchen

being in tune with God
        "He who belongs to God hears what God says."
                John 8:47

confronting those rumors

a mountain ash tree next to my window

energetic people

feasting my eyes on a psychedelic sunset

rest

my willingness to be the best that I can be

a small personal declaration of independence

old friends

_____

_____

_____

cordless phones

peace in the a storm
>"He got up and rebuked the winds and the waves,
>and it was completely calm." Matt. 8:26

letting God enfold me in His arms

everyone

the comforts of home

folk art

easy dinners

being alone with God

enrolling in a class just for fun

blow-dry haircuts

Thanks

light traffic

the words "no cavities"

a hopeful heart

that God rescues me
        "He reached down from on high and took hold of me;
            he drew me out of deep waters.
                He rescued me from my powerful enemy,
                    from my foes, who were too strong for me.
            . . . he rescued me because he delighted in me."
                Ps. 18:16,17,19

being cool, calm and collected even when fiercely opposed

my United States citizenship

escaping temptation

listening to my favorite music

dreams and hopes for the future

_____

_____

_____

thorough documentation

the 119 million acres of forest in Alaska

being given the benefit of the doubt

cinnamon tea

that love is a choice

a sun-dappled place beneath the tree

everyday delights

victory over death
      "But thanks be to God!
            He gives us the victory
                  through our Lord Jesus Christ." I Cor. 15:57

bookcases

the goal of being debt-free
      "Let no debt remain outstanding,
            except the continuing debt to love one another."
                  Rom. 13:8

rosebuds

exceptional customer service

sunlight glowing through new spring leaves
as the cycle of life
promises hope

God's boundless love and mercy

safe driving conditions

early morning walks

a celebration dinner
"Go, eat your food with gladness,
and drink your wine [grape juice] with a joyful heart,
for it is now that God favors what you do."
Eccl. 9:7

choosing to be happy

overcoming my fear

a new foal

bright turquoise

exerting a good influence

saying "no thanks" to dessert

learning to cope in more positive ways

Christian books
"Jesus did many other things as well.
If every one of them were written down,
I suppose that even the whole world
would not have room
for the books that would be written."
John 21:25

breaking a bad habit

functional furniture

_____

_____

_____

expanding my knowledge

that pain won't last forever

a treasured find

bright beautiful threads of joy throughout my life

agreeing on the price

the natural disease-preventing chemicals in fruits and vegetables

eagerly waiting for His coming
      "The friend . . . waits and listens for him,
          and is full of joy when he hears
             the bridegroom's voice." John 3:29

deodorants

victory
      "It was not by their sword that they won the land
          nor did their arm bring them victory;
             it was your right hand, your arm,
                and the light of your face,
                   for you loved them." Ps. 44:3

extra time

detailed notes

enlarging my circle of friends

flowers gently unfolding

the Holy Spirit
      "The Spirit of the Lord will rest on him--
          the Spirit of wisdom and of understanding,
             the Spirit of counsel and of power,
                the Spirit of knowledge
                and of the fear [love] of the Lord--"
              Is. 11:2

escaping a close call

good quality

bringing comfort

the illustration of God's love
        "God demonstrates his own love for us in this:
              While we were still sinners,
                     Christ died for us." Rom. 5:8

season tickets

a cordial greeting

giving my problems to Him
        "Cast all you anxiety on him
              because he cares for you." I Pet. 5:7

the whole sky awash in billowy-soft clouds

facing the reality of my mistakes and letting them go

a creative approach

that in God we trust
        "Some trust in chariots and some in horses,
              but we trust in the name of the Lord our God."
              Ps. 20:7

Thanks

writing poetry

reforming my health habits even in small ways

_____

_____

_____

the eyes -- the mirror of your soul

wholeness

the farmers' market

wide bold stripes

that the long slender dragonfly eats mosquitoes

uplifting words
    "May the words of my mouth and the meditation of my heart
        be pleasing in your sight, O Lord." Ps. 19:14

trying to understand

a corner table in a restaurant

covering the mistake with Liquid Paper

trading an old clunker for a better car

having enough

going home

that God hears my cries
"I love the Lord, for he heard my voice;
he heard my cry for mercy.
Because he turned his ear to me
I will call on him as long as I live." Ps. 116:1,2

having Christ as the center of my life

a burst of energy

looking deeply into a flower

doing a job well
"Be very careful, then, how you live--
not as unwise but as wise,
making the most of every opportunity."
Eph. 5:15,16

breakfast

saftey through the night

expressive phrases

THANKS

that God can make up for lost time
"I will repay you for the years the locusts have eaten."
Joel 2:25

cab drivers

dexterity

golden September days

paved roads
"In all your ways acknowledge him,
and he will make your paths straight." Prov. 3:6

fun and easy things to do

_____

_____

_____

looking carefully at the pros and cons

great ideas

a friend in which to safely confide

ordinary people

THANKS

that depression is temporary
    "Why are you downcast, O my soul?
        Why so disturbed within me?
    Put your hope in God,
        for I will yet praise him, my Savior and my God."
      Ps. 42:11

everlasting life

a meadowlark singing at the edge of a cornfield

faith

unutterable joy in heaven
    "They will enter Zion with singing;
        everlasting joy will crown their heads.
          Gladness and joy will overtake them,
            and sorrow and sighing will flee away."
      Is. 51:11

excellence

familiarity with some of the world's great music

happy days

giving God my best
    "So whether you eat or drink or whatever you do,
        do it all for the glory of God." I Cor. 10:31

Thanks

shopping by catalog

discarding things that dim my vision of God

the privilege of church attendance
> "Let us not give up meeting together,
>   as some are in the habit of doing,
>   but let us encourage one another--
>   and all the more as you see the Day approaching."
>   Heb. 10:25

feeling comfortable

gently waiting and trusting
> "but those who hope in the Lord
>   will renew their strength." Is. 40:31

expanding my horizons

charisma

a gift from a secret pal

following the best course and then just waiting

active listening --
>   someone totally focused on me
>   as if I were the most important
>   person in the world

Thanks

My favorite music and books

THANKS

displays that teach

calendar art

that I don't need to be afraid
  "I will take refuge
    in the shadow of your wings
      until the disaster has passed." Ps. 57:1

freedom from compulsivness

library books

blessed assurance

---

decrying religious intolerance

feeling good about myself

displacing sin
  "Be pleased to accept my advice:
    Renounce your sins by doing what is right."
      Dan. 4:27

Thanks

unmerited mercy
> "The Lord our God is merciful and forgiving,
> even though we have rebelled against him." Dan. 9:9

my firsthand knowledge of God's love

divine help

bluebirds

gift boxes

deep longings satisfied

the greatness of God
> "Great is the Lord and most worthy of praise;
> his greatness no one can fathom." Ps. 145:3

lingering just a moment more

fellow Christians

being willing to be made willing

tall cattails in the marsh

bonuses

doing it myself/asking for help

a clear conscience
      "Let us draw near to God
            with a sincere heart in full assurance of faith,
                  having our hearts sprinkled to cleanse us
                        from a guilty conscience." Heb. 10:22

a new sense of wholeness

listening to the wind

parting that's such sweet sorrow
      sweet -- because we love enough
            to feel the sorrow of parting
                -- I'm thankful for that intensity

filling the tub with instant warm water

a lightweight water-resistant jacket

doing that difficult thing

_____

_____

_____

precious faith
      "Your faith -- of greater worth than gold." I Pet. 1:7

losing five pounds

botanical gardens

a happy face
  "A happy heart makes the face cheerful." Prov. 15:13

explicit guidelines

charging an item that's on sale

the value of knowing Jesus
  "I consider everything a loss
    compared to the surpassing greatness
      of knowing Christ Jesus my Lord,
        for whose sake I have lost all things.
  I consider them rubbish, that I may gain Christ"
  Phil. 3:8

a one-of-a-kind gift

gentle encouragement

someone crossing the room to greet me

unspeakable joy
  "You believe in him and are filled
    with an inexpressible and glorious joy."
    I Pet. 1:8

THANKS

dedicating my life to God

satisfying my heart's hunger

a simple explanation

fire alarms

discernment
"Be wise about what is good
and innocent about what is evil." Rom. 16:19

large sweet dark red cherries

genuinely charming people

sparkling eyes

new excitement in my life

seeds
    sprouts
        roots
            stems
                leaves
                    flowers
                        and fruits

lavishly illustrated books

continuing on in spite of that handicap

someone who has significantly affected my life

_____

_____

_____

answered prayer
      "Let me tell you what he has done for me.
         . . . God has surely listened
             and heard my voice in prayer." Ps. 66:16,19

nibbling at the edges of a big project

my awareness of the presence of God

learning healthier behaviors

self-confidence
      "The fruit of righteousness will be peace;
         the effect of righteousness will be quietness
            and confidence forever." Isa. 32:17

stop and go lights

extra help

THANKS

making a new friend

a few good men

not having to defend my conduct

that He satisfies the empty spot in my life
"The one who feeds on me will live because of me."
John 6:57

calendars

a longing for more of God flooding my heart
"My soul yearns for you in the night;
in the morning my spirit longs for you." Is. 26:9

new truths that were hidden before

finding a feasible plan

stretch denim jeans

ordinary usual regular predictable things

_____

_____

_____

that God desires my companionship
> "Call upon me and come and pray to me,
> and I will listen to you."
> Jer. 29:12

no lines at the check-out counter

sunflowers along the edge of the road

the joy in planning

vindication
> "He will remove the disgrace of his people
> from all the earth." Isa. 25:8

the force of gravity giving shape to the earth

fresh grape juice

great over-arching trees

simplifying

being a survivor

that I am bound to God
> by cords of love

fellow workers

Thanks

unity

 "that all of them may be one, Father,
   just as you are in me and I am in you.
 May they also be in us so that the world may believe
   that you have sent me." John 17:21

a new coat

my enjoyment of life

that our destination is heaven

sitting on the step of the porch

the beginnings of emotional healing

God's mercy

 "Our God has not deserted us in our bondage.
  He has shown us kindness . . .
   He has granted us new life . . .
    and He has given us a wall of protection."
    Ezra 9:9

old acquaintances

selling by consignment

a grove of white birches

slide programs that captivate my attention

God's promise of intimacy
"I will betroth you to me forever;
I will betroth you in righteousness and justice,
in love and compassion.
I will betroth you in faithfulness."
Hosea 2:19,20

our state government

"made in America"

slide programs that captivate my attention

vision
"Lift up your eyes and look about you." Is. 60:4

discovering wisdom

a peaceful era

_____

_____

_____

fun beyond my wildest imagination

packing all my clothes for a trip in only one carryon

THANKS

People for God to bless

_____

_____

_____

_____

_____

_____

_____

Thanks

the balance of nature

finishing it

shoulders

conservation
"Gather the pieces that are left over.
Let nothing be wasted." John 6:12

making the necessary corrections

gaining strength to fight the daily battle

finding the answer

May flowers

soaking in a bubble bath

doing better than I did before

my body's natural production of endorphins

gentle discipline

firmer faith

stars shining in cloudless brilliance

meeting halfway

the way that God draws me to Himself
      "God's kindness leads you toward repentance." Rom. 2:4

a few quiet moments

settling a disagreement

that I believe
      "I do believe; help me overcome my unbelief!"
          Mark 9:24

orange ambrosia salad

the free enterprise system

paying back a loan

meeting expenses

a moment of overwhelming holiness

fleecy clouds
      sweeping across the sky canvas
          brushed there with a feather
             by the hand of God

moving forward with the plans

people who are pleasant and easy to talk to

_____

_____

_____

self-respect
"Each one should test his own actions.
Then he can take pride in himself,
without comparing himself to somebody else."
Gal. 6:4

a quietly-understated suit

having the best that is available

an effective exercise routine

my ability to think logically

physical recovery

joys to come

a grape arbor

motherly or fatherly advice

heroes and heroines
> in the common walks of life
>> whose unselfish motives
>>> classify them equally
>>>> with those who are greatly recognized

plastic bags

mutual trust

that He never gives up on me
> "He will never leave you nor forsake you."
> Deut. 31:6

doing what's right

a glass full of sweet slippery ice chips on a hot day

my calling to be an emissary of Christ's love

the way that He loves
> "I will heal their waywardness
>> and love them freely." Hosea 14:4

drawing in closer

old-fashioned chivalry

my day-to-day activities

God's promises
        "For no matter how many promises God has made,
                they are "Yes" in Christ." II Cor. 1:20

my favorite fruit

_____

_____

_____

for God opening a way
        "See, I have placed before you an open door." Rev. 3:8

comfort and solace in times of grief

a wooded hill

anything of beauty
        its lines, colors, form, texture,
                proportions, rhythms, tones,
                        behavior, features

formal gardens

saguaro cactus standing tall in Arizona

my favorite flannel pajamas

THANKS

doing it graciously

_____

_____

_____

silent unspoken gestures
    of warmth and affection
        between two people

provocative magazine articles

our local government

right motives

sensitivity
    "Rejoice with those who rejoice;
        mourn with those who mourn." Rom. 12:15

drinking fountains

this quiet moment

my own snug bed

quality time

longing for more of God
"As the deer pants for streams of water,
so my soul pants for you, O God." Ps. 42:1

that my love can multiply

reflections in a perfectly still lake

bereavement counseling
"We can comfort those in any trouble
with the comfort we ourselves have received
from God." II Cor. 1:4

the correlation of daily Bible study and spiritual growth

simple ordinary things in life

_____

_____

_____

waking up "on the right side of the bed"
"But I will sing of your strength,
in the morning I will sing of your love."
Ps. 59:16

rainbow colors

passing the exam

high ideals
      "Aim for perfection,
           listen to my appeal,
               be of one mind,
                   live in peace.
     And the God of peace be with you." II Cor. 13:11

a finely crafted limited edition book

adequate compensation

the Bible
      "All Scripture is God-breathed
             and is useful for teaching, rebuking, correcting
                 and training in righteousness." II Tim. 3:16

my favorite chair

Scotch tape

natural products

warmth inside my house
      while gusts of frigid wind
           swirl and sculpt drifts of snow

felt needs being met

reading between the lines

peace as a result of forsaking sin

the wonderful things God has done
  "The Lord has done great things for us,
      and we are filled with joy." Ps. 126:3

hot cinnamon apple cider

realizing a more balanced perspective on holidays

a discount for paying on time

neatly organized material

people who are considerate of others

human companionship

a decisive moment

_____

_____

_____

night lights

THANKS

God's providence
    "You intended to harm me,
        but God intended it for good
            to accomplish what is now being done,
          the saving of many lives."
          Gen. 50:20

forgiving one another

just being myself

serving Christ
    "I tell you the truth,
        whatever you did for one of the least of these . . .
        you did for me." Matt. 25:40

pink grapefruit

Indian summer

my mind

for God
    living and working
        through me

relationships

intimacy with God

Thanks

listening to God
> "If he calls you, say, 'Speak, LORD,
>   for your servant is listening.'" I Sam. 3:9

fresh air

red-winged blackbirds perching on a fence

the years of my life
> "The righteous will flourish like a palm tree,
>   they will grow like a cedar of Lebanon;
> They will still bear fruit in old age,
>   they will stay fresh and green." Ps. 92:12,14

resisting the inclination to criticize

freedom of the press

poignant stories

keeping cool

daring to stand alone

the welcome light of dawn after a long night

a delicate lighter-than-air dandelion puff

cut flowers on the table

THANKS

the Christian influences in our world

_____

_____

_____

fresh hopes

the clock tower on campus or in town

rain-soaked rocks shining in the sun

keeping my relationship with God fresh and alive

that we shall behold Him
        with our own eyes
                face to face
                        intimately
                                personally
                                        individually

dawn's early light

my daily devotions with God

caring people
        "Blessed is he who has regard for the weak." Ps. 41:1

that He is able
"He is able to save completely those who come to God
through him." Heb. 7:25

keeping within my budget

good deeds

simple terms

making ends meet

listening to Christ
"Here I am! I stand at the door and knock.
If anyone hears my voice and opens the door,
I will come in and eat with him, and he with me."
Rev. 3:20

dealing with that difficulty early on

the conversion of light waves into images by my eyes and brain

a crescent moon

fair employment practices

laughing aloud

getting there ahead of time

tender emotions

_____

_____

_____

the fragrance after rain

God's response to prayer
      "As soon as you began to pray,
           an answer was given." Dan. 9:23

the consistency of physical and chemical laws in the universe

a cat purring

funny stories

this day
      "This is the day the Lord has made;
          let us rejoice and be glad in it." Ps. 118:24

getting home safely

having my complaints resolved

standing firm

His soon coming
> "For in just a very little while, 'He who is coming will
> come and will not delay.'" Heb. 10:37

products free of defects

learning new words

the delicacy of a petal

funny bumper stickers

a couple of love birds

the drama of a butterfly emerging from a chrysalis

getting up later

sleep
> "When you lie down, you will not be afraid;
> when you lie down, your sleep will be sweet."
> Prov. 3:24

not always going along with the crowd

the fruit of the Holy Spirit within me
> "The fruit of the Spirit is love, joy, peace, patience,
> kindness, goodness, faithfulness, gentleness
> and self-control." Gal. 5:22,23

freedom from want

courage for tomorrow
      "You will not have to fight this battle. . .
            Do not be afraid; do not be discouraged.
                Go out to face them tomorrow,
                      and the Lord will be with you." II Chr. 20:17

the emphasis of God's love throughout the Bible

just being still for a while

simply being alive

my furniture

a special solitary place
      "Come with me by yourselves
            to a quiet place
                and get some rest." Mark 6:31

the extraordinary fragrance of gardenias

a welcome friend
      "How beautiful on the mountains
            are the feet of those who bring good news,
                who proclaim peace,
                    who bring good tidings,
                      who proclaim salvation." Is. 52:7

THANKS

tax exemptions

sixteen

the fragile beauty of a rose

one time

———————————————————

———————————————————

———————————————————

carrying within me an inward calm despite the hectic world
"Peace I leave with you; my peace I give you.
I do not give to you as the world gives.
Do not let your hearts be troubled
and do not be afraid." John 14:27

soft cotton fleece against my skin

having the courage to counter the bad ideas of others

the gentle breeze
refreshing my spirit
whispering to my soul

new clothes

THANKS

a flat of raspberries

colorful foliage

the fine arts --
        painting
             sculpture
                  music
                        dancing
                              drama
                                     literature
                                          architecture

an awareness of extenuating circumstances

gentle confrontation
        "If someone is caught in a sin,
                you who are spiritual should restore him gently . . ."
                Gal. 6:1

small changes I can make now

_____

_____

_____

fresh-from-the-dasher ice cream

biographies --
         windows into the lives
               of those who have accomplished much

finalizing the whole thing

this tender promise
       "And God will wipe away every tear from their eyes."
         Rev. 7:17

a long walk with a friend

celebrating my freedom in Christ

simple prayers

plants' conversion of sunlight to chemical energy

the variety of wholesome beverages

His careful coaching and counseling
       "I will praise the Lord, who counsels me;
           even at night my heart instructs me." Ps. 16:7

that criminals are brought to justice

soaring to new heights of joy today

words of encouragement

a brand new heart
    "I will give you a new heart . . .
        I will remove from you your heart of stone . . .
    And I will put my Spirit in you."
        Ezek. 36:26,27

the American flag

that wickedness will cease
    "A little while, and the wicked will be no more;
        though you look for them, they will not be found.
    But the meek will inherit the land and enjoy great peace."
        Ps. 37:10,11

soft sweet golden-brown dates

a fair and square deal

willingness to stop some of the hustle
    to take the time
        to drink in
            more of Him

that I'm a valuable human being

solitude
    "Therefore I am now going to allure her;
        I will lead her into the desert
           and speak tenderly to her." Hosea 2:14

THANKS

the glad day when Jesus will come again

a "missing you" card

feeling drowsy at bedtime

unusual out-of-the-way places

_____

_____

_____

sins forgiven
    "Though your sins are like scarlet,
        they shall be as white as snow;
            though they are red as crimson,
                they shall be like wool." Is. 1:18

speaking without pretense

charm

a familiar sight

visiting museums

hymns of triumph

THANKS

the family of God
"Here are my mother and my brothers!
Whoever does God's will
is my brother and sister and mother."
Mark 3:34,35

storms that I have weathered

precision quartz watches

free publicity

the healing process

walking in new and deeper spiritual paths

thoughtfulness
"You broaden the path beneath me,
so that my ankles do not turn." II Sam. 22:37

special meaningful times of prayer

that it's OK because, after all, I'm fallible

a smooth flight

inspirational biographies of spiritual giants

IRA accounts

Thanks

His power to save me
      "He will keep you strong to the end,
           so that you will be blameless
                on the day of our Lord Jesus Christ." I Cor. 1:8

the due process of law

adventure

celebrating everything
        holidays
                birthdays
                    sad days
                        glad days
                          all the time

fringe benefits

a potential catastrophe that didn't happen

_____

_____

_____

the kind of gift that keeps on giving

pine-fringed roads

THANKS

that love is the motive
"For Christ's love compels us." II Cor. 5:14

a cost-of-living wage increase

the exaltation of God forever
"Day and night they never stop saying:
'Holy, holy, holy is the Lord God Almighty,
who was, and is, and is to come.'"
Rev. 4:8

having my hair restyled

wisdom
"The fear [love] of the Lord--that is wisdom,
and to shun evil is understanding." Job 28:28

United States savings bonds

the lavish ways of God's love

singing
"Is anyone happy? Let him sing songs of praise."
James 5:13
a glossy finish

that God holds my hand
"I, the Lord, have called you in righteousness;
I will take hold of your hand." Is. 42:6

thinking about heaven

the look of gentleness on another's face

a frisky puppy

that I am born again

keeping in touch with faraway friends

_____

_____

_____

a new beginning

> "Hide your face from my sins and blot out all my iniquity.
> Create in me a pure heart, O God,
> and renew a steadfast spirit within me."
> Ps. 51:9,10

rich navy blue

total commitment to God

singing in the shower

large old cottonwood trees

 THANKS

forgetting the past
"Forget the former things; do not dwell on the past.
See, I am doing a new thing!
Now it springs up; do you not perceive it?
I am making a way in the desert
and streams in the wasteland." Is. 43:18,19

a book that crackles with humor

the capacity to earn a living
"You may say to yourself,
'My power and the strength of my hands
have produced this wealth for me.'
But remember the Lord your God,
for it is he who gives you
the ability to produce wealth."
Deut. 8:17,18

telling someone I appreciate them

whatever's best

knowing it'll be done on time

sale prices

prayer groups
"For where two or three come together in my name,
there am I with them." Matt. 18:19

THANKS

My freedoms

_____

_____

_____

_____

_____

_____

_____

Thanks

the preciousness of life

laughing more

a considerate employer

saying yes/saying no

a small step in de-emphasizing the importance of material goods

visiting the library

petting the soft nose of a calf or colt

that God will never overlook me
>"Can a mother forget the baby at her breast
>and have no compassion on the child she has borne?
>Though she may forget,
>I will not forget you!" Is. 49:15

shelves full of books

no need to fear
>"The LORD is my light and my salvation--
>whom shall I fear:
>The LORD is the stronghold of my life--
>of whom shall I be afraid?" Ps. 27:1

a favor willingly done

Thanks

three baby birds in a nest
       beaks open so widely
           so expectantly
               so continually

silly moments

_____

_____

_____

keeping the faith

a special person in my life

the homeplace

smiles that let you know everything's all right
       "A cheerful look brings joy to the heart,
           and good news gives health to the bones." Prov. 15:30

friendly terms

that nothing is insurmountable
       "With God all things are possible." Matt. 19:26

a direct answer

listening
> "Therefore consider carefully how you listen."
> Luke 8:18

time in which to consider the consequences

apologies
> "Therefore confess you sins to each other
> and pray for each other." James 5:16

the growing realization of His presence

a sweet fragrance

the daily stuff of life
> "When times are good, be happy;
> but when times are bad, consider:
> God has made the one as well as the other."
> Eccl. 7:14

having someone cater to my needs when I'm sick

a double rainbow

standing on a dock watching the boats come and go

hope for tomorrow

admitting I'm wrong and feeling OK about it

streamlining a cumbersome process

joys in the journey

_____

_____

_____

His happy love songs for me
          "I will sing for the one I love." Is. 5:1

a neat desk

deciding what's important in my life

amazement and wonder at His re-creation in my life

slowing down

traveling

an acceptable standard of living

telephone directories

sharing my real self with others

Thanks

composure
> "Let us then approach the throne of grace with confidence,
> so that we may receive mercy
> and find grace to help us in our time of need."
> Heb. 4:16

no hard feelings between us

a full-bodied stretch

psychological tests

an empathetic counselor

the blessings of reading the Bible
> "Blessed is the one who reads the words of this prophecy,
> and blessed are those who hear it
> and take to heart what is written in it,
> because the time is near." Rev. 1:3

sweet expressions of friendship

pure artesian water

time for personal prayer
> "Jesus often withdrew to lonely places and prayed."
> Luke 5:16

an exquisite little gift

forgiveness
> "'Neither do I condemn you,' Jesus declared.
> 'Go now and leave your life of sin.'" John 8:11

alarm clocks

soup and crackers

constructive criticism
> "Whoever heeds correction gains understanding."
> Prov. 15:32

all my possessions

hidden courage that I didn't know I had

splitting the difference

raising money for an important purpose

an uncrowded place

birthdays
> "Teach us to number our days aright,
> that we may gain a heart of wisdom." Ps. 90:12

allowing God to paint a picture of His love in my life

starting over

THANKS

words that bring tears of joy to my eyes

_____

_____

_____

the anointing of the Holy Spirit

a butterfly garden

softening a cynic's belief that all people are cruelly selfish

taking time out

God's tender care
"I will lead the blind by ways they have not known,
along unfamiliar paths I will guide them;
I will turn the darkness into light before them
and make the rough places smooth." Is. 42:16

wriggling my toes

high fiber foods

quiet contemplation about Jesus

strong bones

THANKS

a special sanctuary of trees
    gilded by rocks and wild flowers
        carpeted by thick pine needles
            orchestrated by musical breezes
                caroled by water spilling over rocks

strength

realizing that sin hinders my happiness

loyalty
    "'Do all that you have in mind,' his armor-bearer said.
        'Go ahead; I am with you heart and soul.'"
        I Sam. 14:7

answers

that our minds feed on what we read

a competent physician

honest communication

the Bible's
    harmony
        beauty
            poetry
                encouragement
                  and direction

summer rain

an irresistible price

pleasant courtesies

_____

_____

_____

appreciation

hospitals

a purpose in life
      "The only thing that counts is faith
          expressing itself through love." Gal. 5:6

concentration in spite of distractions

tact and delicacy

porcelain mugs

art galleries

strolling down a tree-lined street

time to say goodby to one who is dying
>> so at least there is good closure in the relationship

confidence
>> "For God did not give us a spirit of timidity,
>>> but a spirit of power, of love
>>>> and of self-discipline." II Tim. 1:7

a favorable report

the innocence of childhood

having enough energy

my Teacher
>> "Show me your ways, O Lord, teach me your paths;
>>> guide me in your truth and teach me,
>>>> for you are God my Savior." Ps. 25:4,5

assertiveness

centering my life in God
>> "Now all has been heard;
>>> here is the conclusion of the matter:
>>>> Fear [love] God and keep his commandments,
>>>>> for this is the whole duty of man."
>>>>>> Eccl. 12:13

the latest research

Thanks

a subtle blending of colors

talking face to face

automatic garage door openers

the love chapter (I Cor. 13)

a thirst for knowledge

ten minutes in the sunshine

avoiding a fight

the benefits of doing God's will
> "The commands of the Lord are radiant,
> giving light to the eyes.
> . . . in keeping them there is great reward."
> Ps. 19: 8,11

a canopy of stars

tender childlike love

chatting briefly with other shoppers

His love
> "Because your love is better than life,
> my lips will glorify you." Ps. 63:3

Thanks

energy

    "The joy of the LORD is your strength." Neh. 8:10

that a particular danger has passed

_____

_____

_____

that I can be completely open with God

dark green jade

a letter from a friend

tithing/giving

    "Honor the Lord with your wealth,
        with the firstfruits of all your crops;
      then your barns will be filled to overflowing,
          and your vats will brim over with new wine."
        Prov. 3:9,10

fresh blueberries

daylight saving time

the privilege of filing a counterclaim

association with those of like mind
    "Do two walk together
        unless they have agreed to do so?" Amos 3:3

that God melts the clouds of sadness

helium balloons on strings

a reasonable explanation

deciding on the basis of principle rather than feeling

the Holy Spirit's intimate continual presence
    within me
        around me
           everywhere
              always

our earth's cycle of distillation giving us rain

that God is a husband to the single woman and widow
    "Do not be afraid; you will not suffer shame.
        Do not fear disgrace; you will not be humiliated.
    You will . . . remember no more
        the reproach of your widowhood.
    For your Maker is your husband--
        the Lord Almighty is his name." Is. 54:4,5

a sense of humor

making other plans

God's way of leading
      "I led them with cords of human kindness,
           with ties of love." Hosea 11:4

sweet communion with God

the stuff memories are made of

being on a first name basis

daily joy
      "You are to rejoice before the Lord your God
           in everything you put your hand to." Deut. 12:18

the sweetness of life

_____

_____

_____

enlightenment
      "Then he opened their minds
           so they could understand the Scriptures." Luke 24:45

that the formation of my character follows logical laws

THANKS

my personal story or testimony
      "Come and see what God has done,
            how awesome his works in man's behalf!" Ps. 66:5

taking one day at a time

a light humorous essay

the ceaseless ages of eternity

being changed by God from what I read in the Bible

mankind's deep need
      "We would like to see Jesus." John 12:21

a rainbow
      breaking through
          stormy black clouds
              painting a message of love

woods and fields bursting with life

the little white church in the vale

a sweet expression

being equipped to handle it

an artist, author, or composer with a sensitive style

trading our brokenness for wholeness

accepting a compliment graciously

the privilege of praise
"I will praise you as long as I live,
and in your name I will lift up my hands.
My soul will be satisfied as with the riches of foods;
with singing lips my mouth will praise you."
Ps. 63:4,5

a small box of keepsakes

the ability to choose

my response to God
"And when they heard that the Lord was concerned
about them and had seen their misery,
they bowed down and worshiped." Ex. 4:31

small almost unnoticed blessings

_____

_____

_____

a dab of butter on hot vegetables

Thanks

prayer partners
"Then Daniel returned to his house
and explained the matter to his friends . . .
He urged them to plead for mercy
from the God of heaven." Dan. 2:17,18

the sense of touch in my finger tips

soft bath mats

unobstructed drainpipes

witnessing
"Do not be afraid; keep on speaking, do not be silent."
Acts 18:9

a color-coordinated room

the conversion of the power of falling water to electricity

another day

twelve

authors
"My heart is stirred by a noble theme
as I recite my verses for the king;
my tongue is the pen of a skillful writer."
Ps. 45:1

Thanks

changing for the better

mischievous masked raccoons

travel brochures

a box containing all the puzzle pieces

songs that evoke memories

the privilege of consulting an attorney

uncommonly beautiful landscapes

history

> "Remember the days of old;
> consider the generations long past.
> Ask your father and he will tell you,
> your elders, and they will explain to you."
> Deut. 32:7

pearlescent balloons

time

> "My times are in your hands." Ps. 31:15

walking out of the fog

understanding another's needs

THANKS

Reflections

_____

_____

_____

_____

_____

_____

_____

that God is always with me
      everywhere
            every day
                 every moment

the process of digestion

personality contrasts and differences

_____

_____

_____

those who prepare and distribute food

a cheerful note

that God will never leave me
     "Where can I go from you Spirit?
         Where can I flee from your presence?
    If I go up to the heavens, you are there;
        if I make my bed in the depths, you are there.
    If I rise on the wings of the dawn,
        if I settle on the far side of the sea,
   even there you hand will guide me,
       your right hand will hold me fast."
           Ps. 139:7-10

THANKS

billowing clouds

watching a rainbow until it's gone

sitting on the grass under a tree

birthday cards

the Lord's prayer (Matt. 6:9-13)

soft wool

a refreshing night's sleep

that I can know I am saved
      "You may know
            that you have eternal life." I John 5:13

Black gospel music

meteor showers

three things

_____

_____

_____

a drop in prices

boundaries
"The boundary lines have fallen for me
in pleasant places;
surely I have a delightful inheritance."
Ps. 16:6

the national anthem

quality merchandise

my body's circulatory system

lengthening shadows slowly disappearing into the sunset

Someone to emulate
"Be imitators of God . . . and live a life of love,
just as Christ loved us and gave himself up for us."
Eph. 5:1,2

today --
I will hear God's whisper
I will listen to His voice
I will be aware of His presence

practical help

a frivolous diversion after working too hard

togetherness with loved ones in heaven forever
"After that, we who are still alive and are left
will be caught up together with them in the clouds
to meet the Lord in the air.
And so we will be with the Lord forever." I Thes. 4:17

the challenges of today

forgiving
"Do not let the sun go down while you are still angry."
Eph. 4:26

twenty-one

canceled debts

women
"Many women were there, watching from a distance.
They had followed Jesus from Galilee
to care for his needs." Matt. 27:55

unconditional acceptance

compliments
"Pleasant words are a honeycomb,
sweet to the soul
and healing to the bones." Prov. 16:24

the long cozy nights in December

THANKS

a heart filled with joy

understated grey

carrying myself straightly and proudly

trading my bondage for freedom
    "So if the Son sets you free,
        you will be free indeed." John 8:36

the conversion of waves into sound by my ears and brain

a leisurely evening

up-to-the-minute data on almost any subject

that today's the best time to start

_____

_____

_____

a little push in the right direction

the correlation between healthy food intake and vitality

caution in dangerous situations

Thanks

tranquility in my life
"He stilled the storm to a whisper;
the waves of the sea were hushed.
They were glad when it grew calm,
and he guided them to their desired haven.
Let them give thanks to the Lord for his unfailing love
and his wonderful deeds for men." Ps. 107:29-31

casual clothes

a cooperative effort

enthusiasm
"Whatever your hand finds to do, do it with your might."
Eccl. 9:10

the curtain rising on stage

sharing a private personal thought

lightheartedness
"He makes my feet like the feet of a deer;
he enables me to stand on the heights." Ps. 18:33

the privilege of casting a ballot

an unforgettable video

computers

a cheerful voice

the thrill of anticipation

aromatic clusters of lily of the valley

blessings in abundance
   "From the fullness of his grace
      we have all received one blessing after another."
         John 1:16

the relief of a decongestant

concocting a wild mixture that becomes a favorite recipe

a quiet life
   "Make it your ambition to lead a quiet life." I Thes. 4:11

the emotional cleansing of crying

huge bright beach balls

anticipating something wonderful

_____

_____

_____

my Perfect Counselor
"Nothing in all creation is hidden from God's sight.
Everything is uncovered and laid bare
before the eyes of him." Heb. 4:13

the lock on my door

contentment
"For I have learned to be content
whatever the circumstances." Phil. 4:11

a friendly "Good morning"

the sun faintly filtering through the dusky fog

apples

the completeness of an unbroken circle

our civil liberties

triumph at last
"I know that my Redeemer lives,
and that in the end he will stand upon the earth.
And after my skin has been destroyed,
yet in my flesh I will see God;
I myself will see him with my own eyes--
I, and not another.
How my heart yearns within me!" Job 19:25-27

all eternity

breaking out of my rut
       exploring new possibilities
              venturing into new relationships

the floating silent beauty of a hot air balloon

God's attentiveness
       "Before they call I will answer;
             while they are still speaking I will hear." Is. 65:24

the gentle lapping of waves on shore

checking off items on the list

openness to the opinions of others
       "Listen to advice and accept instruction,
             and in the end you will be wise." Prov. 19:20

the disturbance from the Holy Spirit when I sin

a barn party
       singing "You are My Sunshine"
           a bonfire
                a hayrack ride
                   a full moon

Christ's enabling

bare feet on thick soft carpet

the variety of nutritious foods

_____

_____

_____

wooden buttons

a dishwasher

just letting the matter drop

worship
    "Let us be thankful,
        and so worship God acceptably
            with reverence and awe." Heb. 12:28

cherry tomatoes

the beauty of this moment

prayer wrapping me
        in billows of God's love

a nurturing support system of friends

Thanks

My goals

_____

_____

_____

_____

_____

_____

the tenderness of God
> "He tends his flock like a shepherd:
>> He gathers the lambs in his arms
> and carries them close to his heart;
>> he gently leads those that have young."
>>> Is. 40:11

choosing the right product

bus drivers

true freedom
> "Where the Spirit of the Lord is,
>> there is freedom." II Cor. 3:17

soul winners
> "Those who are wise will shine
>> like the brightness of the heavens,
>>> and those who lead many to righteousness,
>>>> like the stars for ever and ever."
>>>>> Dan. 12:3

tears that are forgotten

acting in conformity with my principles

the far-reaching effect of one small good decision

natural organic foods

Thanks

that it took only a few minutes

a thankful awareness of the beauty of nature

the gift of a corsage

shaking the doldrums

the strength of bonds of love

ten

my abilities
> "Each one should use whatever gift he has received
> to serve others, faithfully administering
> God's grace in its various forms." I Pet. 4:10

the grandeur of the mountains

songs of praise
> "They sang praises with gladness
> and bowed their heads and worshiped."
> II Chr. 29:30

that friends are forever

a step-by-step book

beautiful calligraphy

THANKS

new things I want to try

_____

_____

_____

yellow daffodils
      triumphantly blossoming
            in the spring snow

the ability to learn

conviction
      "Were not our hearts burning within us
          while he talked with us on the road
             and opened the Scriptures to us?" Luke 24:32

all the facets of my life

true love
      "And this is love:
          that we walk in obedience to his commands."
        II John 6

a flow of ideas

the clean feeling after washing my hair

Thanks

beating the deadline

that I can give my burdens and problems to God

equality for all
        "There is neither Jew nor Greek,
                slave nor free, male nor female,
                        for you are all one in Christ Jesus." Gal. 3:28

having the oil changed in my car

a dictionary

the evening news

that my essential needs are met

hospital chaplains

making an effort in spite of the odds

complete freedom of choice
        "I have set before you life and death,
                blessings and curses.
                        Now choose life." Deut. 30:19

that the cosmos is a place of order, not a place of chaos

affection

Thanks

a familiar place

_____

_____

_____

daily study
"They received the message with great eagerness
and examined the Scriptures every day
to see if what Paul said was true."
Acts 17:11

the ability to console another effectively

a light dessert

that it was not my fault

browsing in a book store

God's characteristics
"The Lord, the Lord, the compassionate and gracious God,
slow to anger,
abounding in love and faithfulness,
maintaining love to thousands,
and forgiving wickedness."
Ex. 34:6,7

building a bridge over the chasm of misunderstanding

abbreviations

Mary's alabaster box broken for Jesus
     "She has done a beautiful thing to me." Matt. 26:10

that I can brighten my corner of the world

light
     "You are the light of the world." Matt. 5:14

being excused

the church as my extended family

a turning point

_____

_____

_____

buying at a discount

the comforting ticktock of a grandfather clock

a profitable business

THANKS

that He knows the real me
"God does not judge by external appearance." Gal. 2:6

breathing deeply
enjoying the exhilaration
of fresh air

an attractive environment

innocent comedy
"A cheerful heart is good medicine." Prov. 17:22

active busy days

the beginning of a new way of life

buying the best quality

God's will
"He is the Lord;
let him do what is good in his eyes." I Sam. 3:18

the consolation found in debriefing

sharing a compelling book

Mexican food

telling someone "I love you"

a first aid kit

the assurance of salvation

security
       "The eternal God is your refuge,
            and underneath are the everlasting arms."
               Deut. 33:27

belonging

the conviction of the need for change

a familiar song

_____

_____

_____

clear water flowing over round rocks

praying while walking --
      the expansive road Your sanctuary
         the sweeping skies Your cathedral
            the humming trees Your melodies of praise

the gorgeous blending of colors at sunset

eternal life
> "For God so loved the world
>> that he gave his one and only Son,
>>> that whoever believes in him
>> shall not perish but have eternal life." John 3:16

conceiving a better personal plan to witness for Christ

a sense of community within the group

fresh vegetables

_____

_____

_____

buoyancy

the countless opportunities for success in our country

a soul friend
> "Glorify the Lord with me;
>> let us exalt his name together." Ps 34:3

equilibrium

the healing purifying qualities of sunlight

plenty of food
>"Jesus then took the loaves, gave thanks,
>>and distributed to those who were seated
>>>as much as they wanted." John 6:11

helpful suggestions

freedom from guilt
>"Then I acknowledged my sin to you
>>and did not cover up my iniquity.
>I said, 'I will confess my transgressions to the Lord'--
>>and you forgave the guilt of my sin." Ps. 32:5

that He is a God of space and time

being paid double time

the beauty of the earth
>"He has made everything beautiful in its time." Eccl. 3:11

high moral ethics

true wisdom
>"But the wisdom that comes from heaven
>>is first of all pure; then peace-loving, considerate,
>>>submissive, full of mercy and good fruit,
>>>>impartial and sincere." James 3:17

a short devotional

THANKS

hopefulness
>"But as for me, I will always have hope;
>I will praise you more and more." Ps. 71:14

bitter feelings vanished

a peach bursting with juicy flavor

reaching out to others
>"He who refreshes others will himself be refreshed."
>Prov. 11:25

my growing capacity to love more and more

emphasizing the positive

copiers

that I found help

words of healing

_____

_____

_____

bedtime

God's delivery from the bondage of sin

a strong moral character

every situation
> "Give thanks in all circumstances,
> for this is God's will for you in Christ Jesus."
> I Thes. 5:18

a sky washed in lavender and orange

hospice volunteers

Holy Spirit's effect on my life
> "The Spirit of the Lord will come upon you in power . . .
> and you will be changed into a different person."
> I Sam. 10:6

being aglow with love

good directions
> "Whether you turn to the right or to the left,
> your ears will hear a voice behind you, saying,
> 'This is the way; walk in it.'" Is. 30:21

abiding in His presence
> "Keep yourselves in God's love as you wait." Jude 21

blazing red

focusing on my spiritual blessings

_____

_____

_____

that it's worth it to "do life"
"I have fought the good fight,
I have finished the race,
I have kept the faith.
Now there is in store for me the crown of righteousness,
which the Lord . . . will award to me on that day."
II Tim. 4:7,8

a thing of beauty

optimism
"I am greatly encouraged;
in all our troubles my joy knows no bounds."
II Cor. 7:4

our Fathers's compassion for the forsaken
"Do not take advantage of a widow or an orphan.
If you do and they cry out to me,
I will certainly hear their cry." Ex. 22:22,23

being conscious of God's presence right now

Thanks

a walk around the neighborhood

the feeling of freedom in forgiving others

having an equal chance

awe, profound respect and wonder
       at the greatness and grandeur
           of God

correct conclusions

trust instead of fear
       "When I am afraid,
           I will trust in you." Ps. 56:3

weekend getaways

the disease-fighting white corpuscles in my blood

having a good cry once in a while

an autographed copy of a book

satisfaction
       "Godliness with contentment is great gain."
           I Tim. 6:6

the wagging dance of bees as they communicate with one another

Thanks

a concert

God's concern
    "The Lord said, 'I have indeed seen the misery . . .
        I have heard them crying out . . .
            and I am concerned about their suffering.
                So I have come down to rescue them . . .
                    and to bring them up out of that."
                    Ex. 3:7,8

the community college

sound Biblical teaching
    "Pay attention and listen to the sayings of the wise;
        apply your heart to what I teach,
    for it is pleasing when you keep them in your heart
        and have all of them ready on your lips.
    So that your trust may be in the Lord,
        I teach you today, even you." Prov. 22:17-19

being free to love myself and others

recovery from grief
    "He heals the brokenhearted and binds up their wounds."
        Ps. 147:3

the fanfare in heaven when a sinner repents

writing a song or a story

a smile
> "For to see your face
>> is like seeing the face of God,
>>> now that you have received me favorably."
>> Gen. 33:10

breathing prayers
> during all my daily activities

the happiness in giving

CAT scans

welcoming someone new

truth
> "Sanctify them by the truth;
>> your word is the truth." John 17:17

a calm receptive attitude

the conversion of touch by the nerves in my skin and brain

celebrating my spiritual new birth

a spirit of unity
> "May the God who gives endurance and encouragement
>> give you a spirit of unity among yourselves
>>> as you follow Christ Jesus." Rom. 15:5

THANKS

Early happy recollections

_____

_____

_____

_____

_____

_____

center stage

the influence of godly men and women in my life

time to pause and reflect

our country's court system

the availability of the tender
          dazzling
                 powerful
                      joyful
                             love of God for me

a sense of well-being

charitable people

life
        "The Spirit of God has made me;
                the breath of the Almighty gives me life." Job 33:4

the gentle ways of the Holy Spirit

a free gift

the ten commandments
        "I run in the path of your commands,
                for you have set my heart free." Ps. 119:32

charging ahead despite the handicaps

freedom from worry
     "Do not worry about your life,
        what you will eat or drink;
            or about your body, what you will wear.
    Is not life more important than food,
        and the body more important than clothes?"
   "But seek first his kingdom and his righteousness,
       and all these things will be given to you as well."
           Matt. 6:25,33

the eventual victory of all that's good

maturity
     "When I was a child, I talked like a child,
        I thought like a child, I reasoned like a child.
          When I became a man,
             I put childish ways behind me." I Cor. 13:11

old photos

the good habit of saving

reaching out to Jesus
     "Someone touched me;
        I know that power has gone out from me." Luke 8:46

charming Vermont inns

Thanks

that I can try again
    "For though a righteous man falls seven time,
        he rises again,
            but the wicked are brought down by calamity."
                Prov. 24:16

the laws of nature

_____

_____

_____

a positive cash flow

chasing rainbows

tiny treasures

African art

the freedom to worship

plush towels

careful drivers

making a wish and blowing out birthday candles

Thanks

a sense of achievement

_____

_____

_____

devising a new way

the inner ear and its sense of balance

stained glass windows in gothic cathedrals --
        black and bleak outside
                but brilliant and resplendent inside

important aspects of my life

the latest catalog

canned foods

carefully considering all the facts

time to sit down

a walk in the park

the correlation between right thinking and right doing

Thanks

praying --
> God and I abiding in each other
>> so closely that our cheeks touch
>>> as He embraces me

that Jesus lives
> "Before long, the world will not see me anymore,
>> but you will see me. Because I live,
>>> you also will live." John 14:19

calm assurance

barber and beauty shops

dazzling flashes of lightning and peals of thunder

all-in-one casseroles

spiritual renewal
> "The hour has come for you to wake up from your slumber,
>> because our salvation is nearer now
>>> than when we first believed.
> The night is nearly over; the day is almost here.
>> So let us put aside the deeds of darkness
>>> and put on the armor of light." Rom. 13:11,12

the liberating effect of laughter

carryout food

a cherished memory

carrying through the interview with confidence

my intuition

trying it -- and liking it
> "Taste and see that the Lord is good;
> > blessed is the man who takes refuge in him." Ps. 34:8

toll-free 800 phone numbers

emotions and feelings

_____

_____

_____

weekend plans

an extraordinary friendship

the distinct spicy scent of carnations

a favorable impression

winning the chase

THANKS

that He never changes
      "Jesus Christ is the same
            yesterday and today and forever." Heb. 13:8

the gentle, quieting effect of God's presence

caution signs

that we each can do something unique
      "We have different gifts,
          according to the grace given us . . .
            prophesying . . .
              serving . . .
                teaching . . .
                  encouraging . . .
                    contributing . . .
                  leadership . . .
                mercy . . ."
                  Rom. 12:6-8

an open window

sharing an unguarded moment

Bartlett pears

the glad reunion in heaven

a correct assessment of the situation

THANKS

brown gaunt trees
    naked and helpless in winter
        but retaining a secret promise
           of new fresh creation within

sharing the joy

brightly colored ceramic bowls

quietness
    "Be still, and know that I am God." Ps. 46:10

autobiographies of outstandingly faithful people

whatever brightens the day

cutting loose once in a while

that God will get me through difficulties
    "At my first defense, no one came to my support,
        but everyone deserted me . . .
           But the Lord stood at my side and gave me strength,
    so that through me the message might be fully proclaimed."
        II Tim. 4:16,17

saving grace
    "For it is by grace you have been saved, through faith--
        and this not from yourselves,
           it is the gift of God." Eph. 2:8

THANKS

celebrating a graduation

uncrowded airports

the ability to cope
"So do not fear, for I am with you;
do not be dismayed, for I am your God.
I will strengthen you and help you;
I will uphold you with my righteous right hand." Is. 41:10

counting the cost before I decide

optimism for tomorrow

_____

_____

_____

air-drying the dishes

clear acrylic things

the opportunities money brings

a sense of adventure

velcro

praying in the chapel --
      solitude glorified
           by His nearness

the cultural benefits of the city

my little corner of the world
      "Better one handful with tranquillity
      than two handfuls with toil and chasing after the wind."
      Eccl. 4:6

catching up most of my work

all the wild creatures

_____

_____

_____

that maybe it doesn't matter -- after all, God is in control
      "If God is for us, who can be against us?" Rom. 8:31

creating beauty just for the pleasure of it

the right answers
      "A man finds joy in giving an apt reply--
         and how good is a timely word!" Prov. 15:23

Thanks

a free consultation

affordable prices

crunching into a crisp juicy apple

aluminum foil

art reproductions that compare well with the originals

quiet strength
> "In repentance and rest is your salvation,
> in quietness and trust is your strength." Is. 30:15

comfortable furnishings

the assurance of God's love

_____

_____

_____

day-by-day Bible verse calendars

curbing the desire to overeat

ample time

THANKS

C. S. Lewis' writings
     his brilliance
          perseverance
              and intense faith

deep velvety darkness on a moonless night

everything
    "Let the sea resound, and everything in it,
        the world, and all who live in it.
    Let the rivers clap their hands,
        let the mountains sing together for joy."
        Ps. 98:7,8

common ordinary days

an easy-to-approach person

the privilege of knowing Jesus

winning a friendly debate

staying in His presence all day
    "Blessed are those who have learned to acclaim you,
        who walk in the light of your presence, O Lord.
          They rejoice in your name all day long."
        Ps. 89:15,16

average people doing extraordinary things

rejuvenation
     "He will come to us like the winter rains,
         like the spring rains that water the earth."
         Hosea 6:3

complimentary samples

the rhythm of the moon and stars
      night and day
          perfectly timed and tuned
             as a silent symphony directed by God

an exclamation of joy

doing whatever I can

_____

_____

_____

an invitation to dinner

congeniality

deciding

avoiding the full effects of the economic crunch

delight in the Lord
"Delight yourself in the Lord
and he will give you the desires of your heart."
Ps. 37:4

baby Jesus
the Creator King enfolded in humanity
exchanging the throne of God for the manger
relinquishing the friendship of angels for cattle in a barn
surrendering heavenly adoration for the cross
breathing Love to a lonely planet

for God touching me
embracing me
recreating me
healing me
loving me

the power of choice

making my own cross reference system in my Bible

that I can be completely open with God
"But whenever anyone turns to the Lord,
the veil is taken away." II Cor. 3:16

contagious hilarious laughter

a flock of starlings dancing in the sky

THANKS

changing habits and hang-ups
"Being confident of this,
that he who began a good work in you
will carry it on to completion
until the day of Christ Jesus."
Phil. 1:6

enthusiastic clapping

deciphering the meaning of another's body language

a graceful answer

compassion
"When he saw the crowds, he had compassion on them,
because they were harassed and helpless,
like sheep without a shepherd." Matt. 9:36

pets

_____

_____

_____

delicate pansies

whole grain bread

THANKS

meeting the crisis
>with serenity and faith

comprehending the meaning behind the words

satisfying my soul's thirst
>"Whoever drinks the water I give him
>>will never thirst." John 4:14

that I can do it with God
>"He has showed you, O man, what is good.
>>And what does the Lord require of you?
>>>To act justly and to love mercy
>>>>and to walk humbly with your God."
>>>Micah 6:8

continuing in the faith

a deeper fuller sense of His presence

the surety of God's promises and His second coming
>"For the revelation awaits an appointed time;
>>it speaks of the end
>>>and will not prove false.
>Though it linger, wait for it;
>>it will certainly come and will not delay."
>>Habakkuk 2:3

being honest with myself

Thanks

delicatessens

appreciating solitude

God's love for me
> "The Lord your God is with you,
>> He is mighty to save.
> He will take great delight in you,
>> He will quiet you with His love,
>>> He will rejoice over you with singing."
>>>> Zeph. 3:17

a fair-minded person

competence

revival
> "Dry bones, hear the word of the Lord!
>> This is what the Sovereign Lord says to these bones:
>> I will make breath enter you,
>>> and you will come to life.
>> I will put my Spirit in you,
>>> and you will live" Ezek. 37:4,5,14

shelter

the privilege of asking questions

despondency lifting

Thanks

a quiet activity

_____

_____

_____

that we are His children
"How great is the love the Father has lavished on us
that we should be called children of God!
And that is what we are!" I John 3:1

grace
"Where sin increased, grace increased all the more."
Rom. 5:20

that my life can express God's love

feeling better than yesterday

courage in the face of uncertainty

a road with wide curves

dependable love
"Love never fails." I Cor. 13:8

a simple message

Thanks

defending someone else

riches (we all are rich)
"Wealth and honor come from you;
you are the ruler of all things . . .
Now, our God, we give you thanks
and praise your glorious name."
I Chr. 29:12,13

a quiet evening

design artists

finding happiness in new ways

_____

_____

_____

asking questions and receiving answers

balance
"It is not good to eat too much honey,
nor is it honorable to seek one's own honor."
Prov. 25:27

the conversion of gasoline into motion by an engine

THANKS

classical guitar music

being equal to the task

a short commute

dentistry

personal prayer
　　"When you pray, go into your room,
　　　　close the door and pray to your Father." Matt. 6:6

developing my abilities

courage in the struggle

a time of vibrant health

my good characteristics

_____

_____

_____

using clout graciously

doing it first class

Thanks

controlling my temper

a follow-up letter

snow falling softly and silently

steadfastness
        "Never tire of doing what is right." II Thes. 3:13

disarming hostility

brilliant fall leaves frolicking on the grass
        swirling, swishing, whirling, clattering
                kaleidoscopes of color
                        dancing their finale
                                as autumn's curtain closes

craving a closer relationship with God

God's faithfulness
        "The Lord is faithful to all his promises
                and loving toward all he has made." Ps. 145:13

avoiding a fatal mistake

thinking about black holes and the curvature of space

cultivating good work patterns

THANKS

communion -- the wine and the bread
      "And he said to them,
              'I have eagerly desired to eat this Passover
                     with you before I suffer.'" Luke 22:15

irrepressible giggles

apricots

the resurrection
      "For the Lord himself will come down from heaven,
          with a loud command,
              with the voice of the archangel
                   and with the trumpet call of God,
    and the dead in Christ will rise first." I Thes. 4:16

convenience food

art and craft shows in the park

burdens lifting

      _____

      _____

      _____

discretion

salvation
>>"But when he saw the wind,
>>>he was afraid and,
>>>>beginning to sink,
>>>>>cried out, 'Lord, save me!'
>>>Immediately Jesus reached out his hand
>>>>and caught him." Matt. 14:30,31

our sense of direction
>>"I am the way and the truth and the life." John 14:6

snowflakes drifting lazily downward
>>covering the world with purity
>>>softening the harshness
>>>>forming fluffy contours
>>>>>from the Master Sculptor

the release felt from turning my problems over to God

discarding the formalities

that the Holy Spirit is with me
>>"My Spirit remains among you. Do not fear." Haggai 2:5

background music in stores

current data

diversifying and expanding a business

THANKS

a wink and a smile

joyful reunions

making someone's heart glad

_____

_____

_____

sunlight
       streaming through window panes in my room
             on a cold December day

discussing controversial topics amiably

the next-to-the-last page

closeness
       "Come near to God
           and he will come near to you." James 4:8

happiness
       "Now that you know these things,
          you will be blessed if you do them." John 13:17

a deepening appreciation of the beauty around me

THANKS

you
"I thank my God every time I remember you." Phil. 1:3

the last page

friends
"I have called you friends,
for everything that I learned from my Father
I have made known to you." John 15:15

being able to give you this book
"A longing fulfilled is sweet to the soul." Prov. 13:19

Check your local book store
or
AN EXTRA ORDER FORM
TO SHARE WITH FRIENDS!

ORDER FORM

Yes! Please rush me:

_____copies of THANKS $11.95 U.S. Enclose check.
(Please add $3.00 for postage and handling for one book,
$1.00 for each additional book.)

_____ information on fund raising or multiple gift giving

Send this order form with your check to:
TreeTop Books
P.O. Box 486
Nampa, ID 83653-0486

Name _____

Address _____

City _____ State _____ Zip_____